Accountancy for UK Contractors

JAMES RICHARDSON

D1421974

<u>Disclaimer</u>

This book is intended to help directors of small limited companies understand their responsibilities. It is not a complete guide to these requirements and should not replace direct reference to government information or the advice of a qualified accountant.

In all cases the reader is advised to check government resources directly or consult an accountant.

While the information in this book is believed to be correct, no liability can be accepted for any errors or omissions. It should also be noted that the rules applying to companies are constantly changing. It is your responsibility to keep up to date.

This publication mentions, and provides contact details for, a number of organisations. These are provided for the convenience of the reader, should they wish to use the same services as the author. No association with or endorsement of this book by these organisations is implied. Any trade names mentioned belong to their respective owners.

Published by James E Richardson (Electrical) Limited

Copyright © 2017 James Richardson

All rights reserved.

Updated : September 2017

ISBN: 0-9957492-0-5
ISBN-13: 978-0-9957492-0-7

To my Uncle Fred

CONTENTS

ACKNOWLEDGMENTS

With thanks to the Edinburgh Self-Publishing Writers Meetup Group for their advice on producing this book in printed form.

Thanks also to Irina, for her help with payroll journals and my mother, Dorothy, for assistance proofreading.

Appendix A recommends some suppliers I have used myself. These companies kindly allowed me to include their contact details and in some cases, screenshots.

1. INTRODUCTION

After being made redundant I took a contracting job which required me to set up a limited company. Without any accountancy training I registered my business, appointed an accountant, arranged insurance and bank facilities, created a website and maintained proper accounts throughout my first year of trading.

With a good understanding of finance and maths plus plenty of real world experience I assumed this would be straightforward.

Unfortunately that was not the case. Accountants train for many years and now I understand why. Search online and you will find many brief guides to running a business. Run your business for real however, and things are more tricky. Suddenly those internet articles can seem very superficial.

Even with the help of an accountant it took me several months to understand my accounts. I started sharing this hard won information on my website but soon had so much that I put together this book.

The aim of this publication is not to train you in accountancy. It is a quick guide to registering a limited company and maintaining its accounts. While it is based on my experience as an electrical contractor it will be useful for anyone starting and running a small limited company in the UK, particularly where they are the only employee.

STRUCTURE OF THIS BOOK

For completeness this book starts with the concept of a limited company. Don't stop reading if you already understand this. I understood the concept of limited companies too but soon hit plenty of problems which I'll describe in later chapters.

Next I describe the process of starting your company, set out your options for accounting and bookkeeping and introduce concepts such as the director's loan account. I give examples of common transactions using QuickFile accounting software but these examples should help you understand any accounting system. Then I'll explain Value Added Tax (VAT), covering the different schemes available and their practical implementation.

With the basic concepts covered we move to the more exciting subject of how to pay yourself from your company's coffers. I'll describe the different types of payment and how to do each in practice. Some thornier subjects come next. I'll cover the dreaded IR35 (disguised employee legislation) and the widely ignored subject of invoicing expenses properly.

With the routine operations complete we move to the year-end by discussing end of year accounts, Annual Confirmation Statements and individual self-assessment.

That covers everything I've learned about business accounts and I'll finish with some final thoughts but before I do I've included a useful bonus chapter on setting up your own website. Like accountancy this is not impossible but is significantly harder than you might expect.

2.   OVERVIEW

WHAT IS A LIMITED COMPANY?

Imagine John is an electrician who wants to work for himself. He could register with Her Majesty's Revenue and Customs (HMRC) as self-employed. He chooses a trade name for his business and is classed as "self-employed". His money and the company's money are not separate. If he loses money he is personally responsible for any debts. He could lose his personal savings and his house. A business with this structure is called a "sole trader".

An alternative arrangement exists in the UK. This is a "private limited company". John sets up his company as above but this time he registers it with Companies House and adds the word "Limited" or "Ltd" to his company name.

The limited company has several shares. All of them are owned by John. It has one employee - John, and his job is "Director", a special class of employee that is involved in controlling a company.

John's friends still describe him as "self-employed" because he does not have a boss but this is technically wrong. In the eyes of the law he is an employee of his company although, as a director, some special rules apply to him.

One advantage of a limited company is that investor's risk is limited. If John's company runs out of money it will be closed down. He will lose his job and any money he invested but his personal assets cannot be claimed by his bank or unpaid suppliers. Another advantage is that a company is not a person so can never have employee's rights, like sick pay or maternity leave. When a business customer contracts work to a limited company they avoid worrying about these things.

John does not have to own all the shares himself. Perhaps his brother gave him £3000 to buy his van and in return his brother has some shares. In this case his brother will receive a share of the profits but does not work in the business. Shares can be sold but they are not listed on a stock exchange.

A different class of (usually much larger) company have names ending PLC (public limited company) and these are the ones traded freely on the stock exchange. Other arrangements are partnerships (similar to a sole trader), limited liability partnerships and companies limited by guarantee.

In this book I am only interested in private limited companies with one director who is also the main shareholder. I assume the director is the only employee, although most of the information will apply to larger companies too.

The following lists give you an idea of the tasks John must face as director of his own limited company.

STARTING UP

- John registers his company with Companies House.

- He must inform Her Majesty's Revenue and Customs (HMRC) that he has started trading.

- To pay his Corporation Tax he obtains a Unique Tax Reference (UTR) number for his company.

- As a director he must also register for self-assessment of his own personal Income Tax. He obtains another UTR number. This one is for himself as a person.

- Assuming he decides to register for Value Added Tax (VAT), he registers for this with HMRC.

- He needs to pay himself wages. For this he must register for Pay As You Earn (PAYE) with HMRC.

- As director he must record the company's finances. He could pay an accountant or do this himself.

- In case a few of the houses he wires burn down, John takes out "professional indemnity insurance". He also takes out "public liability insurance" in case he injures a member of the public. If he had any employees then "employer's liability insurance" would be a legal requirement.

- Since John's money is separate from the company's he sets up a bank account in the company name.

RUNNING THE COMPANY

- Suppose John gets an order for some electrical work. He agrees with the customer to charge £10000 (excluding VAT).

- John buys some cable and other materials. He pays for these from the company's bank account and records the purchase.

- On completion of the work he prints out an invoice and sends it to the customer. This shows the cost as £10000 + £2000 (VAT at 20%) for a total of £12000. The invoice meets all HMRC's requirements for a correctly produced VAT invoice. John records the issue of the invoice in his accounts.

- Within an agreed period (for example 28 days) the customer pays £12000 into the company's bank account. John records this in his accounts. Note the payment includes £2000 of VAT. This is real money which will sit in the company account until it needs to be given to HMRC.

- At the end of the month John wants some wages. He decides to take £2000 this month. He (or his accountant) notifies HMRC and calculates the correct amount of tax and National Insurance. He pays himself the money from the company's account. He also transfers the tax owed to HMRC.

- Every three months John must complete a VAT return. He pays HMRC the VAT he has collected from customers, minus an allowance for the VAT he has paid on materials and other purchases.

AT THE END OF THE YEAR

- John must complete the company's Annual Confirmation Statement This updates Companies House on non-financial details, for example, the names of the company's directors.

- John (or his accountant) must produce and file the annual accounts. By taking the company's money received (turnover) and subtracting expenses (cost of materials, John's salary) the money left is the company's profit. Corporation Tax (at a rate of 19% from 1st April 2017) must be paid on this. John (or his accountant) must calculate how much tax is owed and send HMRC the money.

- If the company has made a profit, John has the pleasant task of allocating this money. He could leave it in the business or he could pay it to shareholders as their reward for holding shares in the company. If John is the only shareholder this payment will go to him. If his brother owns some shares the money paid is divided between them.

- As a company director, John must register for self-assessment and submit a tax return, even if his earnings are low enough to be a basic rate taxpayer.

UMBRELLA COMPANIES

Hopefully these lists give you an idea of what is involved in running your own business. I've actually glossed over a lot of the complexity. Don't be put off however! It's not impossible and you can pay an accountant to do some of the work for you.

Suppose you get a 12 month contract from a large client who insists they will only deal with a limited company. (They don't want to be saddled with any claims for employment rights.) One option is to work as director of your own limited company. That is what I do and it is the main focus of this book. An alternative, however, is to work through an "umbrella company".

An umbrella company employs various contractors and you would be one of its employees should you take this route. You are not a director of the company and therefore need not worry about the accounting described in this book.

Advantages of working through an umbrella company

- You don't need to worry about registering a company or recording accounts. You are just an employee.

- You don't need to worry about IR35.

- The umbrella company may save you costs such as insurance and accountancy fees.

Disadvantages

- You will pay more tax.

- The umbrella company will take a cut of your fees.

- You are not in business for yourself and miss out on the experience and opportunity of being your own boss.

- You may find your scope for claiming expenses reduced.

- You are still a contractor and miss out on the perks and security of permanent staff.

An umbrella company is less effort, especially if you only expect to work as a contractor for a short time. Setting up a limited company is more suitable if you want to go it alone longer term and potentially build up some sort of business.

ACCOUNTING OPTIONS FOR YOUR LIMITED COMPANY

Assuming you want to work as boss of your own limited company, you have four choices:

Full service accountant

You record everything in a spreadsheet and let your accountant sort it out. Most people do this. Remember that the director is ultimately responsible for the accounts, not the accountant. You will pay about £1500 + VAT a year, depending on how much you do yourself and what extras are thrown in (for example insurance or IR35 reviews).

Own bookkeeping and budget accountant

You can do the routine bookkeeping yourself. Your accountant advises you and compiles the annual accounts.

This is how I run James E Richardson (Electrical) Limited. I record all transactions directly into online accountancy software. I calculate and submit my own VAT returns. At the end of the year my accountant produces my annual accounts. He also does my monthly payroll calculations, although I record these and move the money. I produce the Annual Confirmation Statement for Companies House.

This arrangement involves much more work but has two big advantages - it's cheap (I pay £540 + VAT a year) and you learn how everything works.

Be prepared to spend many hours studying online. You will do most of the work yourself, but with the accountant as a back-up when you get stuck.

Check and file only

Do almost everything yourself with no advice, including preparation of the annual accounts. At the end of the year you pay about £150 for an accountant to check your accounts and submit them.

Do everything yourself.

There is no law that says your business (at least if it's small) has to have an accountant.

Now you know what a business must do the next section will cover getting started.

3.   STARTING YOUR LIMITED COMPANY

People love to tell you how easy it is to register your own company. You pay £15, wait a few hours, and there you are - the next Microsoft!

Unfortunately this is not really true. A few hours and fifteen pounds will indeed get you a certificate with your new company name. Once you get your certificate however, there is a lot more to do before you can meet your legal obligations as director to record accounts and pay taxes. In this chapter I'll explain the various start-up tasks.

REGISTRATION

Pick yourself a nice name. Check you can get a matching website address.

Find yourself an online agent that registers companies. The package I purchased was aimed at contractors and cost £50. I particularly wanted:

- PAYE registration
- VAT registration
- A bank account with a £50 cash back deal.

There are many registration firms so you can compare the cost and features of their various packages. You can also register direct with Companies House but using an agent is both cheaper and easier.

You must decide how many shares your company has and their nominal value. I chose to have a single, £1 share. If your company has several owners you would choose a larger number, for example 24 or 100, which is divisible many ways.

Shares can be paid or unpaid. My £1 share is unpaid and should my company go bust I would be personally liable for £1. Paid up shares allow you to put money into the company without being owed it back. Unless you have a good reason (typically involving other people investing or lending money) you can just leave your shares unpaid and give your company any money it needs as a loan.

For one, or even a hundred, unpaid shares your liability is tiny. Do not get carried away however and register a million unpaid £1 shares just because you can. You might regret it if things go wrong.

You can register a company by yourself. There is no need to have other directors, shareholders or a company secretary. You are required to display a sign at your premises but this does not apply if the premises are a residential home.

You must provide a registered address for your company. If you use your own address it is displayed by Companies House for every scam artist and direct marketer to see. Alternatively you can use a forwarding address, for example a solicitor. This costs about £50 per year with the first year free. I didn't hide my address and have had no problems or junk mail.

A somewhat daft rule is that your company is registered in either Scotland, England & Wales or Northern Ireland. This is determined by your registered address. If you register your business to your house in Scotland, then two years later move to England, you cannot change the registered address to your new home. You must either pay a solicitor in Scotland to register you at their offices for £50 a year, or close down your company and register a new one in England.

On registering you will receive some emailed documents including a certificate with your company's registration number.

BANK ACCOUNT

The next task is to set up a bank account in your company's name. My registration included a business bank account with a high street bank and £50 cash back when I opened it. These cash back schemes effectively make registration via a formation company free so there is little reason to do it yourself through Companies House.

Check details of charges (there is often a free period of 12 - 18 months), whether you will get a debit card (I didn't get one and now manage without) and if you can register for internet banking straight away.

I set up my company in a hurry as I was working away from home. I had to register for internet banking after the account was opened when it would have been more convenient for me to have done this at the initial meeting.

ACCOUNTANT AND ACCOUNTANCY SOFTWARE

Next choose your accountant. The more you pay the less you need to be involved. Many people just fill in all their transactions on a spreadsheet for the accountant to deal with. In this book I describe my set up which involves me doing all of the bookkeeping and arguably some of the accountancy.

I use a budget accountancy company costing £45 + VAT each month, which is very cheap. For this I get a named person who is my accountant. I can email or phone him but not visit since his office is not local. For that he answers my many questions and does my accounts at the year-end. He also does my payroll and submits RTI (Real Time Information) to HMRC each time I pay myself wages.

The first thing he asked when I signed up was which accountancy software I wanted to use. My needs are basic so I chose QuickFile because it is free. I had also read that using a more advanced package than you need creates extra work. My accountant then set up the software, which is cloud based so he can also see my accounts. QuickFile is very intuitive and has help files but I had to teach myself how to use it. Customer support for QuickFile is via discussion boards but I have received helpful answers through these very quickly from the official QuickFile support staff.

VAT AND PAYE REGISTRATION

I wanted to be registered for both of these. In each case my company formation agent emailed me a form to complete. On returning the forms I was sent login details to HMRC's website. You must then enter this to complete your registration. I believe my accountant would have handled a lot of this for me (even with the basic level of accountancy I have paid for) but I had already done it myself.

You cannot register for PAYE more than 28 days before your first wages. This is because, after registration, HMRC expect wages (even if they are for zero amount) to be declared at planned intervals.

After registering for these schemes you will receive your VAT registration number and PAYE number.

UTR NUMBERS

You may be asked for Unique Tax Reference (UTR) numbers. There are two of these. You have one as a person because you pay Income Tax under the self-assessment system and your company has one because it pays Corporation Tax.

When you register your company, HMRC should send you your company's UTR number. In practice, they frequently don't. If you do not receive it you need to call **0300 200 3410** and ask for it to be posted to you.

Be prepared to spend a lot of time on hold and be passed between various people who confuse your company's UTR number with the more common personal UTR number. Unfortunately there is no other way to get it.

As director of a company you must also register for self-assessment, even if you are a basic rate taxpayer. You don't need to worry about this until after the end (5th April) of the tax year in which you became a director. My accountant registered me. Keep records of your earnings for the year (from 6th April) in which you became a company director.

STARTING TRADING

You are required to tell HMRC that you have started trading. Just registering at Companies House is not sufficient since it is possible to create a company which is "dormant". It was never clear to me how to do this. If I was starting a new company again I would phone HMRC and ask, just to be sure they had it on record that I was trading.

INSURANCE

There are three main types of business insurance:

- **Professional indemnity insurance** covers mistakes you make - bad work, poor advice.

  Although not compulsory, your customer may require this and it provides protection if you make an expensive mistake.

  It also looks good for IR35 since needing insurance shows your company is exposed to risks in a way employees are not.

- **Public liability insurance** covers injury to members of the public. It is not compulsory.

- **Employer's liability insurance** covers injury to your employees. If the only employee is you, and you are a director, you do not need it. Otherwise it is a legal requirement.

I wasted considerable time on insurance so I can save you from doing the same. Bear in mind that I was looking for insurance to cover work in dangerous industrial environments. Your insurance needs may be different.

The first thing I did was talk to my bank and was told they could not give a quote until after I had the bank account set up. Stupidly I wasted a week waiting for them, only to find they are just agents and couldn't insure me anyway.

The second thing I did was contact insurance companies I'd heard of and asked to be put through to their business insurance section. This got me long phone conversations and huge emailed forms to fill in. The work involved and the estimated prices would be appropriate if you were insuring a factory with 500 workers but completely inappropriate for my little company with just me.

Finally I contacted some companies who specialised in contractor insurance. These had plans matching my company's size and the type of work I was doing.

I paid £500/year for a package with £1m professional indemnity, £5m public liability and some other useful insurance thrown in. This was a straightforward package and no more complicated than car or house insurance.

That's the initial set up finished. In the next chapter we start on the accounting.

4.   BASIC BOOKKEEPING

A proper understanding of double entry bookkeeping is not something you will learn over a weekend with a couple of library books. What I will give you instead is an explanation of the main accounts and transactions I use. I am basing my examples on the free software, QuickFile. This hides some of the bookkeeping complexity and the only time I struggled was with the journal entries needed to record payroll. If you use different software it will probably operate in a similar manner.

ACCOUNTS

There are hundreds of accounts within the workings of QuickFile, each with a nominal code number, for example 1200 (current account). Except for payroll, I have managed to avoid worrying about most of these and let QuickFile sort things out. The two exceptions, which you must understand before going further, are the current account and the director's loan account.

The current account is simple. It is the amount of cash in your newly opened business account at your high street bank. If your current account contains a value of +£100 then your company has £100 in the bank that it could spend. If the current account is minus £100 then your company owes the bank money (an overdraft).

The director's loan account is more complex but very important. If it contains +£100 then the company is owed £100 by the directors (ie, you!). In a similar way to the +£100 in the bank this means the company owns £100 which it could potentially get one day and spend. If the director's loan account is minus £100 it means the company owes the directors money. This is analogous to the bank overdraft but in this case the company has borrowed from the director's personal savings.

Remember that the director's loan account is not a record of the director's money. It is record of the amount of company money deposited with (or borrowed from) the directors. Typically the current account is positive (unless you have deliberately borrowed from the bank) and the director's loan account is negative (the company will often owe you money but unless you have a special reason to borrow from it you would not normally owe money to the company).

DIRECTOR'S LOAN ACCOUNT IN ACTION

Some examples will clarify how this useful account works in practice.

Suppose your company has £100 in its current account and the director's loan account is zero. You purchase a screwdriver for £3 using the company debit card. The current account is now £97.

The director's loan account is still zero and the company's total cash is £97 + 0 = £97.

Alternatively you might have been in a hurry or not had a company debit card. Instead you buy a screwdriver from a local tool store with your own money, using a five pound note in your pocket. You keep the receipt and need to enter the transaction in your accounts.

In this case the company has still spent £3 (the screwdriver was for the company, not you) but instead of reducing its current account the company has increased its debt towards its directors. You would record this in the accounts as a purchase paid from the director's loan account. Since the director's loan account started at zero it falls to minus £3. The current account is unchanged. Accounts are now:

Current account:	£100
Directors Loan account:	- £3

You can see that the company's total cash is still the sum of these at £97. It is as though the company has an account at two different banks, one of them run by the director with his own money.

At a later date you may decide you want your £3 back. To do this, pay £3 from the company's current account to your personal bank account. Record this as a transfer between company accounts of £3 from the company's current account to the company's director's loan account.

The accounts will now be:

Current account:	£97
Directors Loan account	0

This is the same as if the company had just bought the screwdriver directly. Note that this final transfer is just a movement between the company's two accounts. The money actually left the company's balance sheet earlier when the tool was bought using the director's loan account.

RECORDING PURCHASES WITH QUICKFILE

If your business makes a purchase you should have a receipt or invoice. Otherwise you might just be helping yourself to company funds without paying Income Tax and National Insurance on what would effectively be wages.

QuickFile has a nice system for receipts. You tell QuickFile the email addresses you will be sending receipts from. Then you just email a scanned or electronic copy to **receipts@quickfile.co.uk**. QuickFile takes the attachments, identifies your company from your email address, and loads them into the receipt area of your account. If there is no attachment it assumes the email body is the receipt.

Next time you log into QuickFile and go to "Receipt Hub" you will see copies of the receipts. For each one you enter the value (including VAT) and the date. You will be asked if you want to create a new purchase order. Click "yes" and mark "paid in full". You should then select "paid from director's loan account" (if you paid with your own money) or "paid from current account" (if you paid from the company current account).

QuickFile will then record the purchase, store an electronic copy of the receipt and adjust the current account or director's loan account balance. You need to actually pay the money to the supplier. QuickFile only records the transaction. If everything is done correctly the current account in QuickFile should match the company bank balance and the director's loan account should be negative by whatever amount you are personally owed.

RECORDING SALES IN QUICKFILE

When your business sells something it normally issues an invoice. This does not apply to low value retail sales where different rules apply. To create an invoice, go to the "sales" tab and select "create new invoice". Enter details, noting that you can have either item lines (charged per unit) or time lines (charged per unit of time). QuickFile forces you to choose one time unit for all sales so you cannot charge some invoices by the hour and others by the day. For this reason I usually use "per item" invoicing lines, charging 5 days as 5 units.

If you work through an agency you may find they self-bill. This means they send you invoices recording your sales to them. In this case I create my own invoice (so QuickFile can record the sale amount) but never send it. Instead I attach the agent's self-billed invoice to mine using the upload file facility (available after you save and click "preview invoice"). I then select "flag invoice as sent" which updates the records but does not send the invoice to anyone.

Figure 1. The "New Invoice" screen in QuickFile

TRANSFERS BETWEEN ACCOUNTS IN QUICKFILE

After recording expenses, your company's director's loan account will build up a negative balance representing money owed by the company to you. Every so often you will decide to collect this money.

Select "current account" from the banking menu. Then select "make payment" and "transfer between accounts". Choose "transfer to director's loan account" and make a matching payment in the real world from the company account to your own personal account.

You might do the opposite if your company is short of money. When starting your business it may be several months before you are paid for work. In this case you can pay your own money into the business and record this by making a transfer from director's loan account to current account.

LOANS

Take care not to accidently make the director's loan account positive. If you wish your company to lend you money you should study the tax rules. This is particularly important if you carry a loan over the company year-end.

IMPORT AND TAG BANK STATEMENTS

It is possible to import your bank statements and then let QuickFile help you tag these and match them against receipts. I have not bothered with this but it may save you time if you wish to use it.

RECEIPTS

If you travel by rail be particularly careful to get proper receipts when paying in person. Always ask for a "business receipt". If you just ask for a "receipt" you may be given a debit card sales receipt which is not the same thing.

Taxis are another tricky item since some firms are VAT registered and some are not. I work on the assumption that if the receipt (often resembling a business card with a scribble on one side) contains a VAT number then the firm is VAT registered and the amount contains VAT at 20%.

This is important if you register for VAT yourself, which is the subject of the next chapter.

5.   VAT BASICS

If you are in business and don't understand VAT, you could be costing yourself money. In this chapter I will explain how VAT works and the advantages and disadvantages of being VAT registered. The following chapter covers the practical details of administering your company's VAT registration and returns.

WHAT IS VAT?

Value Added Tax (VAT) is a tax levied by HMRC on goods and services sold in the UK. For most things it is charged at 20%. Large companies (based on turnover value) must register for VAT. For very small companies it is optional. Once a company is registered it must charge an additional 20% on everything it sells. It then passes this money to HMRC. The purpose of VAT is to raise money for the government.

Some sales transactions are between businesses. VAT must be charged on these as well. To prevent an item being taxed multiple times, a VAT registered business can claim back the VAT they pay on purchases.

Suppose a shop buys a table from a furniture maker for £100 + £20 VAT. It then sells it to Joe Public for £200 + £40 VAT. When the furniture shop submits its VAT return it will give HMRC the £40 VAT it collected, minus the £20 it paid in VAT to the manufacturer. The end result is that HMRC receives the entire £40 VAT on the table, £20 from the shop's VAT return and £20 from the manufacturer's VAT return.

Why should I get involved?

Small businesses have a number of VAT options. The lower your turnover the more options you have. Each of these choices will result in a different amount of money in your pocket. You need to choose the option that best suits your particular business, taking into account the different administrative burdens. You have three main choices:

- Not VAT registered

- VAT registered on the standard scheme

- VAT registered on the Flat Rate Scheme

NOT VAT REGISTERED

This is the simplest option. Just forget VAT exists. You do not add VAT to your sales prices. For anything you buy you pay VAT, just like a private citizen. It is the best deal if your customers are not VAT registered, for example individual people or non-VAT registered businesses.

VAT REGISTERED ON THE STANDARD SCHEME

This is compulsory for large companies but optional for smaller ones. You charge VAT on all of your sales. When you submit your VAT return you pay this VAT to HMRC minus all of the VAT you have paid on your purchases. It is the best deal (unless your trade has a favourable flat rate under the Flat Rate Scheme) if your customers are VAT registered and you buy a lot of materials.

VAT REGISTERED ON THE FLAT RATE SCHEME

This is an interesting option, popular with small businesses whose customers are VAT registered but who buy few materials, for example consultants advising large businesses. HMRC devised this scheme as a low administration alternative to the standard scheme.

On the Flat Rate Scheme you charge full VAT to your customer but only pay a fixed percentage of your turnover to HMRC rather than the full amount of VAT collected. Suppose you are an engineering consultant and bill your customer for £1000 + VAT. You would charge your customer full VAT at 20% and receive £1200 when they paid the invoice.

If your flat rate was 14.5% you would pay 14.5% of the £1200, which is £174, when you submit your VAT return. The spare £26 you get to keep as a mysterious extra profit. It is as though you sold your services for £1026+VAT. If your customer is a VAT registered business they can still reclaim the £200 VAT that they paid so it makes no difference to them. As a consultant this would give you a 2.6% pay rise on every hour that you bill.

It seems that the taxman is subsidising your wages out of his own pocket. Is this a mistake, black magic, aggressive tax evasion or just simple VAT fraud? Actually it is none of these. On the Flat Rate Scheme you do not claim anything back from your purchases, despite charging VAT on your sales. The £26 is meant to approximately cover the VAT you pay on your purchases without the administrative effort of calculating it properly. Different flat rates are allowed for different types of business. A builder supplying their own materials would get a low rate because they pay a lot of VAT buying bricks and timber. A consultant gets a less favourable rate because they buy less things and are mostly selling their time.

Note that the flat rate is applied to the VAT inclusive amount of £1200, not to the ex-VAT price of £1000.

Limited Cost Traders

The Flat Rate Scheme is an approximation intended to reduce bookkeeping effort.

Calculating a percentage of your turnover every three months is easier than adding up the VAT component of every purchase under the standard scheme. HMRC have set the rates for different trades and provided you pay a typical amount of VAT on your purchases the "profit" from the Flat Rate Scheme should roughly cover it.

Naturally small business owners are not stupid. If they have unusually low input VAT they will be very keen to use the Flat Rate Scheme. Should they have high input VAT they may accept the administrative effort of the standard scheme, rather than make a loss.

On £50000+VAT turnover at 14.5% you would make a flat rate "profit" of £1300. Unless you buy £6500+VAT of goods and services at 20% you will gain. In practice it is easy to spend quite a lot. Accountancy fees and frequent accommodation or vehicle costs will soon eat into this amount. Overall though, it is a generous scheme which could be argued as helping small businesses with both less administration and a subsidy of several hundred pounds a year.

Unfortunately in the 2016 Autumn Statement a change was announced. From April 2017 a new flat rate of 16.5% will be introduced for "limited cost traders".

Limited cost traders are defined as those who spend less than a set amount on "goods". This amount is 2% of turnover or £1000 per year (whichever is higher). This calculation is done at the end of each VAT period.

The change is being billed as a tax evasion measure which is not really fair. The definition of goods excludes food consumed by employees, vehicle fuel and services. The input VAT on all of these items could quite legitimately be claimed via the standard scheme at the cost of extra administrative work. To block potential loopholes, "goods" excludes capital purchases and things you intend to give away.

Since Flat Rate VAT is applied to the VAT inclusive amount, the 16.5% rate means you will receive a negligible refund of your input VAT.

16.5% of £120 is £19.80 - so on every £100+VAT invoiced you would receive 20 pence to cover your input VAT.

HMRC's website has now been updated with guidance and an online tool to determine if you should use the new rate. At least the guidance seems quite clear. Gas and electricity are classed as goods but other borderline items are excluded.

The likely effect will be as follows:

- Limited cost traders with significant input costs not classed as "goods" would be better moving to the standard scheme.

- Limited cost traders below the VAT threshold might choose to stop being VAT registered.

- Limited cost traders above the threshold for VAT registration, or who wish to remain registered because it pleases their business customers, could continue on the 16.5% rate.

Administration is simple but they will lose out each time they pay VAT on a purchase.

- Those not classed as limited cost traders, can continue using the Flat Rate Scheme as before.

VAT notice 733 on HMRC's website covers the Flat Rate Scheme. For more detail on the limited cost trader legislation and a link to the online tool you should see section 4 of this notice. Section 4.5 of this explains how to handle a VAT period that includes months before and after 1st April 2017.

EXTRA COMPLICATIONS

There are two extra things to be aware of:

- **Different VAT rates** - Not everything has VAT at 20%. Some items are 5%, 0% or exempt. Many travel items, for example rail tickets, include no VAT.

- **Cash or accrual accounting** - With cash accounting you owe VAT once a customer pays you. With accrual accounting you owe VAT as soon as you issue the invoice.

WHICH VAT OPTION IS BEST?

If you exceed HMRC's thresholds for turnover your choices are restricted. The current threshold requiring some form of registration is £85000 (from 1st April 2017). Assuming your turnover is low enough to have a free choice, you should consider the following:

- If your customers are not VAT registered you are better off unregistered as well. Registering will add 20% to all of your prices which they cannot claim back.

- If your customers are VAT registered then they can claim back the VAT so the extra 20% on your prices is irrelevant to them. In this case (apart from the extra admin) you are better off VAT registered so you can claim back the VAT on your purchases.

- If you decide to be registered you should consider the Flat Rate Scheme. In some circumstances it will cover the VAT on your purchases and even give you a small profit. For your first year you also get a bonus of 1% off your flat rate! If you buy a lot of materials however, it may cost you a fortune. It is simpler to operate than the standard scheme. From April 2017 there may be no point choosing the Flat Rate Scheme if you are a "limited cost trader".

- Being VAT registered projects an image of a larger, more professional company and, for IR35 compliance, provides additional evidence that you are a real business.

- Being VAT registered can make it more complicated to charge travel and subsistence expenses to a customer.

- Beware of items that carry low or zero rates of VAT. These could drastically affect your profit or loss under the Flat Rate Scheme.

6.   VAT IN PRACTICE

If you decide to register for VAT, this chapter will explain the practical aspects of registering and submitting returns.

HOW TO REGISTER

My VAT registration was included in the company formation package I purchased. The formation agent sent me a form to complete and submitted it to HMRC on my behalf. I then had to complete my registration on HMRC's website at the following address:

https://online.hmrc.gov.uk/registration/newbusiness /introduction

This website is rather confusing at first and asks questions which are sometimes hard to relate to your situation.

If not already registered for HMRC online services you will set up a Government Gateway business account during the registration process. This is used to submit and pay VAT returns. Your username is a long (12 digit) number which you will be told to write down amid warnings it will not be shown again.

I found my company formation agent very helpful during this process but you could also register direct on HMRC's website or via your accountant.

Ultimately you need to end up with two things, a VAT number for your company and login details for HMRC online services (a Government Gateway business account) to allow you to submit your returns.

VAT ON TRANSACTIONS

From the date of your VAT registration you must charge VAT on all of your sales.

Should you decide to register on the Flat Rate Scheme you must choose your flat rate using the guidance notes on HMRC's website (VAT notice 733 section 4). Unfortunately the category names might not match your trade. Unless your business exactly fits one of the categories you must use your best judgement.

A lower rate will make you more money, unless HMRC think you've picked the wrong one, in which case they will decide whether it's an honest mistake or a case of pushing your luck.

For the first year of VAT registration (not necessarily the first year on the Flat Rate Scheme) you should deduct 1% from your flat rate as bonus from HMRC for newly registered businesses (VAT notice 733 section 4.7).

From the 1st April 2017 the "limited cost trader" legislation may discourage many firms from using the Flat Rate Scheme since they must choose the 16.5% rate unless they spend a significant amount on goods.

VAT SETTINGS IN QUICKFILE

In QuickFile you must enter your VAT number if VAT registered. Doing this unlocks extra features so that you can include VAT on your invoices and submit VAT returns. QuickFile even understands the Flat Rate Scheme.

After entering your VAT number you will need to tell QuickFile your other VAT settings.

The example below shows VAT on the Flat Rate Scheme with VAT periods starting March, June, September and December (ending May, August, November and February).

The default of "cash accounting" has been selected which means VAT becomes due at the time invoices are paid, rather than when they are issued. You must enter your chosen flat rate as a percentage for the type of business you are in. For your first year discount you must manually enter a value 1% lower. QuickFile does not do this for you.

Figure 2.   VAT settings in QuickFile

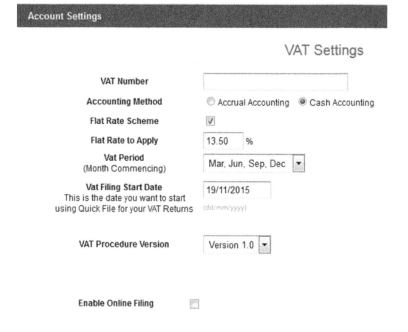

If you are VAT registered you should check the HMRC rules on VAT invoices to ensure you comply. VAT invoices must include the following:

- Invoice number. You must issue consecutive numbers with no unexplained gaps.
- Your VAT number
- Date
- Name and address of both you and the customer
- Quantity, price and VAT rate for items supplied
- Total with and without VAT

For low cost retail sales different rules apply.

VAT RETURNS

VAT returns happen every three months on the last day of the month. If you register for VAT from a date in the middle of a month then your first VAT period will be three and a bit months. Every company's VAT period is therefore one of three options:

- Ending last day of January, April, July, October
- Ending last day of February, May, August, November
- Ending last day of March, June, September, December

After the last day of your VAT period has passed you have a month plus one week to submit a return using HMRC's website and pay any money owed. This is actually quite simple using accounting software such as QuickFile.

Provided your invoices (including recording payment), purchases and VAT details are up to date the reports option in QuickFile will create a table as shown below:

Figure 3.   VAT report figures from QuickFile ready for submission to HMRC

VAT Return

SUBMITTED : 09/03/2016 20:26:23

Cash Accounting (Flat Rate @ 13.5%)		
Date Range From 19/11/2015 To 29/02/2016		

VAT due on sales and other outputs	1	£1,747.17 ▼
VAT due on EC acquisitions	2	£0.00 ▼
Total VAT due	3	£1,747.17 ▼
VAT reclaimed on purchases and other inputs	4	£0.00 ▼
NET VAT to be paid to Customs	5	£1,747.17 ▼
Flat rate turnover inc VAT	6	£12,942 ▼
Total value of purchases exc VAT	7	£0 ▼
Total value of supplies to other EC states exc VAT	8	£0 ▼
Total value of acquisitions from other EC states exc VAT	9	£0 ▼

The above table shows sales of £12942 (£10785 + £2157 VAT at 20%) on which 13.5% (the flat rate) equalling £1747.17 must be paid to HMRC for this period. Notice in this case the business makes a "profit" of £409.83 (£2157 - £1747.17) which is intended to cover the cost of VAT on the business' purchases.

If the company was registered on the standard VAT scheme then the exact cost of VAT on purchases would be deducted instead. The numbers 1 to 9 in the boxes correspond exactly to those on the HMRC website. This website includes helpful explanations, so it is not difficult to print the figures from

QuickFile and enter them online correctly. It is also possible for QuickFile to send the figures automatically but I felt happier typing them myself.

Once you have submitted your VAT return you can print a receipt.

The deadline for payment is the same as for the return, a month and a week from the period end. You must allow time for the payment to reach HMRC.

The easiest way to pay is to set up a direct debit. Be very careful if you use this method. You must register to pay by direct debit several days before submitting your first return or the system will not work and you'll miss a VAT payment.

Details of the time to allow between setting up your direct debit and filing your VAT return are explained when you log in to the online services section of HMRC's website. If you have any concerns it is worth phoning the HMRC VAT people (**0300 200 3700**). They are surprisingly helpful.

7.   PAYING YOURSELF

The purpose of running a business is to earn a living so at some stage you need to get money out. There are three main ways:

- Expenses
- Wages
- Dividends

Expenses reimburse you for money spent on behalf of the company. If you buy a rail ticket out of your own pocket you can move that amount from the company bank account to your own with no tax. You just need to prove you actually spent the money and that it was a valid business expense.

Wages are payment for your employment as a company director. You pay Income Tax and employee's National Insurance on them. Unfortunately your company also pays employer's National Insurance on the amount so in some ways you are being taxed twice.

Paying wages is fairly complicated since you must submit data and payments to HMRC at regular intervals using the new Real Time Information (RTI) system

Dividends are payments to shareholders of the company. They can only be made from company profits. Before making a dividend payment you must calculate your profit and allow for any tax owed.

The advantage of dividends is that, although the company pays Corporation Tax (at almost the same rate as Income Tax), there is no National Insurance. Dividends used to be tax free for basic rate taxpayers but recently an extra 7.5% tax has been introduced.

There are a few other ways to take money. Your company could make payments into a pension scheme as an employer. You could also borrow money from the company as a director's loan but be careful to tax this correctly.

When taking money from your company you must follow the rules carefully or HMRC might decide the payment represents wages or a loan and expect you to have paid tax accordingly.

PAYING EXPENSES

You can be reimbursed tax free for expenses you incur as an individual on behalf of your business.

First you must ensure that the purchase is a valid business expense. The main things that cause confusion are meals and travel.

Valid expenses

You may claim travel expenses to a temporary place of work. Temporary is defined as up to 24 months. It ceases to be temporary from the moment you expect it to be above 24 months, even if this is, for example, after 18 months.

Even if you work at a location for less than 24 months you will not be allowed to claim expenses if it is your normal place of employment. If you are caught by IR35 you will be unable to claim travel expenses to your main workplace since you are classed as an employee. Different clients in the same town may be classed as one location by HMRC (see Employment Income Manuals EIM32080 and EIM32089 at www.gov.uk).

If you are away on business at a remote site then you can also claim for meals. Since you normally eat food, even if not working, this is to compensate you for the extra expense of a meal in a hotel or on a train. If you buy a sandwich on the train you could reasonably claim. Buying food the day before you travel to make your own sandwiches would just be feeding yourself and not a business expense. (see Employment Income Manual EIM31815 at www.gov.uk)

Some items (entertaining, drinks beyond a single beer with your meal, etc) are not valid expenses. For anything borderline I suggest you consult HMRC's guidance notes or ask your accountant.

Recording expenses in your accounts

If you pay bills direct from your company account, things are simple. Just create a purchase order in QuickFile. Ensure you can explain at a later date why that pub lunch was related to your business and keep receipts.

If you pay from your own money you should record the payment as being from the director's loan account. This will result in the director's loan account becoming more negative, showing that the company owes you money.

For mileage in your own vehicle create a supplier "Approved Business Mileage" and record a purchase invoice to that supplier. Be sure to include the number of miles, the rate used in the calculation and the reason for your trip. HMRC's website gives the latest rates, currently £0.45 per mile for cars and vans claiming less than 10000 miles a year.

At this point, documenting of the expenses is almost complete. You just need to get your hands on the money.

When your director's loan account has built up to a sufficient balance you can transfer this amount of money from the company current account to your own account. There is nothing complicated needed to document this. Just record it in QuickFile as a transfer between accounts, from current account to director's loan account.

In a sense you are just moving money between two accounts which belong to the company when you do this, not moving money out of the company. Your business now has less money in its current account but the money in its director's loan account has increased from a negative number to zero so its total assets remain the same.

PAYING WAGES

Expenses should only be covering costs you incur. One way to get money out of your company as reward for your work is a salary. To do this you must register your company with HMRC for PAYE (Pay As You Earn).

To register I completed a form supplied by the agent who registered my company. Alternatively you could register direct on HMRC's website or your accountant could do it for you. You do not need to register until you are ready to pay some wages. In fact you cannot register until 28 days before your first payday because, once registered, HMRC will expect payroll returns at regular intervals. You must make these even if the return is for an amount of zero. My return is on the last day of each month. The day of the month is fixed when you register but the amount can be varied.

New rules require employers to provide workplace pensions. If you are a director and the only employee you can opt out of this via The Pensions Regulator who will write to you.

Before paying wages you must calculate the Income Tax and National Insurance. My accountant does this. Each month he submits the Real Time Information (RTI) to HMRC and sends me pay slips together with the amount I need to pay. This also includes the HMRC sort code, account number and payment reference to use for the payment. If you do not use an accountant there are basic tools on HMRC's website to do this yourself.

From the date the wages are due, you have 22 days to transfer the money to HMRC. I do this by bank transfer and at the same time transfer the net pay to my personal account.

Recording payroll in your accounts

Accounting for payroll is the hardest piece of accounting I have had to do. At first I just transferred the money from the current account in QuickFile. Unfortunately this is wrong. If you do this then your profit and loss account will not be right when you calculate your dividends and Corporation Tax.

To record it properly you need to create journal entries. I will explain how I do this in QuickFile. The method I use requires both wages and tax to be paid on the same day. Should you wish to pay your wages as soon as they are due and wait up to the allowed 22 days to pay the tax then this is also possible but the journal entries are slightly more complicated. To fully understand what is happening you will need to learn about double entry bookkeeping which is a subject in itself. So far I have managed with only the techniques described below.

First decide your gross pay. Calculate (or get your accountant to calculate) the Income Tax and National Insurance owed.

In this example I show how to pay and record a director's gross monthly salary of £2000 assuming tax amounts (from your accountant or HMRC's tool) are as follows:

Employee's gross salary: £2000
Employee's Income Tax: £216.80
Employee's National Insurance: £160
Employer's National Insurance: £184

From the above:
Employee's net pay   =2000-(216.80 + 160) =£1623.20

Amount paid to HMRC = 216.80 + 160 + 184   = £560.80

Cost to company   = 2000 + 184   = £2184

You should pay £1623.20 from the company's bank account to the employee's personal account.
You should pay £560.80 from the company's bank account to HMRC, with the correct payment reference so they know it is from you.

You then need to enter a journal entry in your accounting software as follows. The comments in [ ] brackets are for explanation only - don't type them.

In QuickFile go to "Chart of Accounts" and select "create a new journal entry". You will need to add additional lines to include all the items. The totals for the credit and debit columns must be equal and QuickFile will not allow you to save the journal entry until they are.

The titles "debit" and "credit" are a convention of double entry bookkeeping but do not try to guess which column an entry should be in by using the English language meaning of "credit" and "debit". Just copy the positions shown.

Name of Journal	January 2016 Salary		
Account	Description	Debit	Credit
(1200) Current Account	Net Salary		1623.20 [The net amount paid into the employee's bank account]
(1200) Current Account	HMRC PAYE		560.80 [Total payment to HMRC this month]
(7001) Directors Salary	Jan 2016 Salary	2000.00 [The gross salary before tax]	
(7006) Employer's National Insurance	Employer's National Insurance	184 [Employer's National Insurance]	
Total		2184	2184

If done correctly the current account will be reduced by £2184 and the £2184 will also show up as a cost in your profit and loss account. If instead you just paid your salary and taxes as transfers from the current account then they would not show properly.

Your profit and loss account would actually record net pay as an expense when it should record gross pay, giving an incorrect profit.

Handling rebates

Don't worry if the previous journal entry is complex. In my first year it was my trickiest accounting problem and you'll soon get used to it. Recently I used a more complex version which is useful to know. It was required to handle a tax rebate.

For a large part of the year I paid myself a fixed monthly salary. In November I reduced this to a low level of £600 a month. PAYE Income Tax is based on your pay so far, assuming this rate continues for the rest of the year. Reducing your pay during the year therefore entitles you to a rebate. If the change is small then the next month your tax will be reduced to a much lower than normal amount but no special accounting is needed.

In my case the reduction was so large that the tax owed in the next month was actually negative. The example below shows how this works and is based on two consecutive months.

Rather than enter a negative number (QuickFile does not accept them in journal entries anyway) the amount paid to HMRC is moved from the credit to the debit column. Another nominal code (1101 Sundry Debtors) is used to store the rebate owed by HMRC until the next month when enough tax is owed to cancel it out.

Since the £8.66 is owed to the company by HMRC but not paid (HMRC don't pay you rebates each month) the Sundry Debtors account records the debt while still allowing the current account to match the real current account balance at your bank. You can even see the debt as an asset on your balance sheet.

November 2016

Gross salary:	£600
Income Tax (refund):	-£63.40
Employee's National Insurance:	£28.80
Employer's National Insurance:	£25.94

From the above:

Employee's net pay = 600 - (-63.40 + 28.80) = £634.60

Amount owed to HMRC = -63.40 + 28.80 + 25.94 = -£8.66

Company current account reduced by: £634.60

Amount paid to HMRC this month: £0

A balance of -£8.66 is carried forward to the next payroll and shown as 1101 (Sundry Debtors) in the accounts.

The journal for this is as follows:

Name of Journal	November 2016 Salary		
Account	**Description**	**Debit**	**Credit**
(1200) Current Account	Net Salary		634.60 [The net amount paid into the employee's bank account]
(1101) Sundry Debtors	HMRC PAYE refund	8.66 [Amount owed by HMRC to the business]	
(7001) Directors Salary	Nov 2016 Salary	600 [The gross salary before tax]	
(7006) Employer's National Insurance	Employer's National Insurance	25.94 [Employer's National Insurance]	
Total		634.60	634.60

December 2016

Gross salary:	£600
Income Tax (refund):	-£63.40
Employee's National Insurance:	£72.00
Employer's National Insurance:	£82.80
HMRC balance from November:	-£8.66

From the above:

Employee's
net pay: $600 - (-63.40 + 72.00)$ $= £591.40$

Amount paid
to HMRC: $-63.40 + 72.00 + 82.80 - 8.66$ $= 82.74$

Company current
account reduced by: $591.40 + 82.74$ $= £674.14$

1101 (Sundry Debtors) is now zero. There is no balance with HMRC to carry forward

Name of Journal	December 2016 Salary		
Account	**Description**	**Debit**	**Credit**
(1200) Current Account	Net Salary		591.40 [The net amount paid into employee's bank account]
(1101) Sundry Debtors	HMRC PAYE		8.66 [Credit balance from previous month]
(1200) Current Account	HMRC PAYE		82.74 [Total payment to HMRC this month]
(7001) Directors Salary	Dec 2016 Salary	600 [The gross salary before tax]	
(7006) Employer's National Insurance	Employer's National Insurance	82.80 [Employer's National Insurance]	
Total		682.80	682.80

National Insurance rules for directors

National Insurance has both lower and upper limits which assume an employee is paid similar amounts each week.

Since directors control their own pay they could cheat the system by paying their whole salary for the year in one week. They might also lose out on National Insurance stamps because of other irregular payment patterns.

To avoid these problems there is a special National Insurance scheme for directors.

Under this scheme you pay zero National Insurance until your total wages in the year reach the allowance. After that you pay National Insurance on the rest.

Contrast this with PAYE Income Tax or the National Insurance scheme for non-directors. With these you are allocated a twelfth of your allowance each month (for monthly pay) and it is assumed your wages stay constant. This spreads your tax out more evenly throughout the year but means you pay too much if your wages fall during the year, requiring a rebate in later months or at the year end.

You may notice the increasing amount of National Insurance from November to December in the previous journal examples. This is the effect of being registered on the director's scheme for National Insurance.

Employment Allowance

Small companies used to receive an exemption from paying the first £2000 of employer's National Insurance contributions but this was removed in April 2016 for companies with one employee who is also the director.

Businesses with more employees may still be eligible for this relief which is now increased to £3000.

How much should I pay myself?

A nice problem to have and not too complicated. For the 2017-18 tax year the allowances are as follows. For more detail and a comparison with 2016-17 see "Tax and tax credit rates and thresholds for 2017-18" on the **www.gov.uk** website.

Income :   £11500 tax free then 20% for basic rate

Employee's NI: £8164 tax free then 12% basic rate
falling to 2% for higher rate

Employer's NI: £8164 tax free then 13.8% for both basic
and higher rate

Dividend tax: First £5000 dividends tax free then 7.5%
(Falling to £2000 in 2018-19)

These figures are just for general guidance. For exact calculations use a payroll tool or figures from HMRC's website. This is particularly important with the NI allowances which are stated as weekly amounts.

From these allowances you have a few options (unless forced by IR35 to pay almost everything as salary). The basic concept is to make use of the tax free allowances but pay most of your earnings via the more tax efficient dividend route. Your options are:

- Pay £8164 per annum and avoid paying any National Insurance. Provided you earn at least the equivalent of £113 a week (the "Lower Earnings Limit") your wages still qualify towards a state pension despite you making no National Insurance contributions.

You are potentially wasting your Income Tax allowance but with the new dividend tax you can still use it to save 7.5% on some of your dividends. The attractiveness of this option shows just how large the 25.8% total NI contributions are compared to the more well-known 20% for Income Tax.

- Pay about £11500 per annum to use your Income Tax allowance. Less tax efficient but compared to dividends you are still saving 19% Corporation Tax, even though you are paying 25.8% in National Insurance contributions on part of your wages.

- Pay more than £11500 per annum. Far less tax efficient, particularly as you are paying 13.8% employer's NI contributions which normal employees do not have to pay.

  While your salary level is not relevant to your IR35 status, some argue a higher salary makes it less worthwhile for HMRC to investigate you and gives you less tax to pay back should you later be deemed "inside IR35".

Obviously your personal situation could be far more complicated with other sources of income, a different personal allowance or the effects of hitting the higher rate tax bands to take into account.

PAYING DIVIDENDS

When a company makes a profit the owners of the company are entitled to receive that profit. The way they receive it is a dividend. If you own all the shares in the company then all dividends paid will go to you and this can provide a tax efficient alternative to wages. This is a common situation for one person contractors.

Should you have other large shareholders then dividends will be divided amongst you in proportion to your share holdings. In this case you would generally take a wage which fully compensated you for your work. The dividend would then reward the shareholders for their financial investment in the company.

To pay dividends you must follow strict rules. Dividends can only be paid out of profits so you must work out your profit and then subtract an allowance for Corporation Tax. Once you have worked out your distributable profit you can declare a dividend up to this amount. Take more and it is an "illegal dividend" which HMRC may insist should be taxed as wages or a director's loan.

You do not have to take the full amount as dividends. You could leave the profit in the business to invest, to continue paying wages when business is quiet or to pay dividends at a future time, perhaps in a different tax year. Sometimes however, it is advantageous to take as much as possible. This situation may occur at a year-end, particularly if your personal circumstances have changed or before a change in tax laws. Alternatively you might just need the money.

Calculating distributable profit

To calculate the distributable profit, first calculate your profit by producing a profit and loss statement. QuickFile will produce this as a report. If your company is new, calculate from the time you started. In later years you will allow for the profit carried over from previous years

Having produced your profit and loss account you should print it out and try and understand it. Look at the turnover (money coming into the business). This should cover all invoices issued (even if not yet paid) because your business has earned that money. Equally the expenses should include costs incurred (even if not paid yet) and the cost of gross wages paid.

If your wages are missing, or the cost of Income Tax paid on them is not included, it is a sign that you are not recording your payroll correctly. I had this problem when I tried to pay wages as a transfer directly from the current account, rather than through journal entries.

If you are happy that your profit and loss account is generally correct you will notice there are still some things missing. There may be items which are known, but not yet recorded. Suppose you invoice your customer at the end of each week. If you calculate your profit and loss on a Wednesday and you have worked Monday and Tuesday then you know you will be paid for these days. You will need to make an adjustment by adding an amount for "work in progress".

If you are on the Flat Rate VAT Scheme then you will see your Flat Rate Scheme "profit" as an amount in turnover labelled "Flat Rate VAT sales adjustment". In QuickFile this is only calculated up to the last VAT return. You can calculate this profit on all the invoices (and un-invoiced work in progress) which had not yet been paid on the date of your last VAT return and add it in manually.

Be careful to understand at what point the VAT is recognised. I am on the Flat Rate Scheme using cash accounting for VAT. This means the VAT return only includes invoices which were *paid* on the date of the VAT return. This differs from the inclusion of invoices in the company's profit which occurs as soon as the invoices are *issued,* and even includes the value of work done for which it is expected an invoice will be issued in future.

I use the QuickFile figures for turnover and expenses as a starting point then document the adjustments on a single page in a spreadsheet to give a corrected value for pre-tax profit.

Subtracting Corporation Tax from this pre-tax profit then subtracting any previous dividend payments gives me the maximum dividend payment allowed. I print (and save) this adjustment calculation together with a print out of the profit and loss account it is based on. This provides evidence that I have not issued an illegal dividend.

Note that from 1st April 2017 (not the 5th April) Corporation Tax is 19%, reduced from the previous rate of 20%. Unless your company year ends on 31st March you will have one year that spans both periods. For this you must calculate the number of days at each rate and create a weighted average for the rate. Even if most of your invoices are in the 20% part or the 19% part of the year, you still calculate the tax as though your earnings were steady, based only on the total profit for the year and the number of days at each rate.

The following is a (fictitious) example of the calculation sheet and notes I produce, based on the old rate of 20%. The profit and loss account it would be attached to is not shown here.

Calculation of allowed dividend 4 November 2016

Note 1   The Flat Rate VAT sales adjustment in QuickFile only covers closed off VAT periods. Invoices issued but not paid by last VAT return on 31st August total £9900 (inc VAT) which will give a further Flat Rate adjustment of £313.50.

Note 2   At the time the profit and loss statement was produced there was work completed valued at £500 which had not yet been invoiced. This will result in a further £19.00 Flat Rate adjustment.

Total turnover (from attached Profit & Loss)	28101.00
Further flat rate adjustment for invoices issued but not paid by last VAT return	313.50
Work completed but not yet invoiced	500.00
Further flat rate adjustment on work completed but not yet invoiced	19.00
Revised Turnover	**28933.50**

Less cost of sales

Total cost of sales (From attached Profit & Loss)	600.00
Gross Profit	**28333.50**

Less Expenses

Total expenses (From attached Profit & Loss)	11900.00
Profit before tax	**16433.50**

Less tax

Corporation Tax at 20%	3287.70
Profit after tax	**13145.80**

Year to date dividends	5 April 2016	3450
	25 June 2016	5000

Available to distribute as dividends	**4695.80**

Issuing the dividend

Once you know your distributable profit you can declare a dividend up to a maximum of this amount. Issuing a dividend is straightforward but there are some very bureaucratic procedures which you must follow.

You can issue an "interim" dividend at any time, provided you have sufficient profit. You cannot, however, backdate to a time in the past and make a payment based on your profit at that date. Your calculation and dividend declaration must be now. Dividends paid during the year are called interim dividends. A dividend paid at the end of the year is a final dividend.

Since your company's year may not coincide with the personal tax year (which begins on 6th April) you can arrange to receive the bulk of your dividends in whichever personal tax year most suits you. I pay dividends roughly every 3 months.

To declare your dividend you must have a board meeting and take minutes. This may seem daft if it is just you having a meeting with yourself but that is the law.

I have a template from my accountant to record my meeting minutes. You could easily make one yourself or find one online. It just needs a few sentences to record the following:

- Date of meeting
- Directors present
- Name of company
- Address where the meeting took place
- The fact that an interim (or final) dividend was declared
- The date that the dividend will be paid

- The date shareholders must be on the shareholder register to be eligible for the dividend
- The amount per share of the dividend
- Signature of director(s)

Having had your meeting and written your minutes you must then issue all of the dividend recipients (possibly just you) with a voucher. They will need this to complete their tax return.

Again, you can obtain or make a template. You need:

- Date
- Company name
- Name of person receiving the dividend
- Amount of the dividend
- Signature of director(s)

After all this is done, moving the money is simple. Just transfer from the current account in QuickFile as a transfer out. Mark the transaction as a dividend from the drop down menu. Make a corresponding real world payment from the company's bank account to the dividend recipient.

The following are examples you could copy. If your shares have a nominal value other than £1 (You will have set this value when you formed your company) then replace "£1 ordinary share" with the nominal value you used.

EXAMPLE BOARD MINUTES AND DIVIDEND VOUCHER

Board minute

Minutes of a meeting of <COMPANY NAME> held at <ADDRESS> on <DATE>.

Present: <NAMES OF DIRECTORS PRESENT>

It was decided that the company pay a dividend of £xxx.xx per £1 ordinary share on <DATE> to the shareholders registered on <DATE>

<signature>
< DIRECTOR'S NAME >

Dividend Voucher

<COMPANY NAME>   <DATE>
<COMPANY ADDRESS>

To: <RECIPIENT'S NAME>
     <RECIPIENT'S ADDRESS>

Interim dividend of £xxx.xx per £1 ordinary share for the year ended <DATE OF COMPANY YEAR END> to shareholders registered on <DATE>

<signature>
<DIRECTOR'S NAME>   Director

Number of shares	Dividend Payment
<xx> shares	£<Total payment>

---

8.   IR35 EXPLAINED

IR35 is a set of rules which prevent an employee pretending to be a business to avoid tax. If you are the only person in your company and do a lot of work for one customer you should study the IR35 rules with care.

WHY DOES IT EXIST?

About fifteen years ago crafty people discovered a big loophole in the UK tax system. An ordinary employee pays Income Tax at (currently) 20% and National Insurance at 12%. Their employer pays employer's National Insurance at 13.8%.

A practice emerged where employers and employees colluded to reduce the tax they paid. The employee would resign (or often retire on a good pension) and then return to work the next week as a contractor having set up a limited company. They did a similar job for the same company but now only paid Corporation Tax (currently 19%) and received dividends rather than wages. Not only did they avoid National Insurance but could benefit from timing the money they took from their company to minimise tax and possibly classed a few things as business expenses.

Their former employer saved the 13.8% employer's National Insurance contributions, reduced their number of employees (on paper at least) and freed themselves from a whole host of employment legislation - pensions, sick pay, future redundancy liabilities... No doubt the scheme was promoted by some sort of financial adviser who made a fat cut from the whole thing. A win, win, win situation, for everybody except the poor old Chancellor!

HOW DOES IR35 WORK?

The government's answer was IR35 which forces "disguised employees" to pay taxes like an employee.

There are three principle tests:

- **Substitution** - If your customer pays for an electrical engineer and, while they might get you, you could just as easily send someone else, then you are not an employee.

- **Mutuality of obligation** - If your customer has to keep finding things for you to do and you have to keep doing them then you are an employee. If you stop getting paid as soon as the task is finished then you are a real business.

- **Control** - Does the customer tell you how to do your work? In that case you are an employee. Do they have a job they want done and you decide how to do it? That suggests you are in business for yourself.

If any one of the above results in you being classed as a non-employee then that is usually sufficient to avoid being caught by IR35. In addition:

- **The overall picture is important.** - Is your business obviously a real business in spite of the above? How much do you spend on marketing?

> Do you have a website? Do you have multiple customers at the same time? Are you registered for VAT? Do you risk making a loss if a job goes badly? Can you make extra profit if things go well? Are you "part and parcel" of your customer's organisation?

Note that your lack of employee rights is not an indication of being outside of IR35. The fact you do not get sick pay or a pension does not prove you are a non-employee. Beware of the opposite though. HMRC would take receiving such benefits as a strong indicator that you are.

If you are an "office holder" in your customer's organisation this may also override some of the IR35 tests and allow HMRC to rule that you are an employee.

What happens if I'm "caught" by IR35?

If you are classed as an employee under IR35 two bad things happen.

- You must pay 95% of your revenue as salary. The remaining 5% is meant to cover expenses such as accountancy fees. You are also restricted on things like travel expenses. If you do not pay sufficient salary then at the end of the year you must make a "Deemed Payment" to HMRC as a substitute for the Income Tax and National Insurance they would have got from wages.

- In forcing you to withdraw all money as salary you may find it difficult to run your business as an actual business.

Note that, even inside IR35, you can still make pension payments instead of some of the wages.

SO AM I CAUGHT?

This is the big problem. If you play it safe you will mess up your chance of running a real business and pay a huge amount of tax. Not only do you pay employee's National Insurance of 12% but you will have to pay employer's National Insurance of 13.8% on top, without the job security, sick pay or other perks that employees (who only pay the 12%) would get.

On the other hand, should HMRC decide to investigate you and deem you inside IR35, you could face a huge bill for unpaid tax, possibly with interest and extra penalties.

Neither option is very good so you need to make the best decision you can and hope you are right. I can suggest four things to reduce the risk:

- Study the rules to decide if IR35 applies to you.

- If you think it does not apply then take positive steps to structure your business so there is less doubt.

- Pay a lawyer or accountant for their professional opinion.

- Take out some form of insurance against being investigated or even caught.

Reducing the risk that IR35 could apply

If you are outside IR35 but still worried, there are many positive steps you can take which help demonstrate you are in business on your own and not an employee.

Here are some ideas:

- Work for multiple customers, especially if you can have several contracts at the same time

- Obtain fixed price work, rather than day rate

- Register for VAT

- Invoice for expenses instead of using employee type expenses forms

- Take out professional indemnity insurance

- Ensure your contract is written with IR35 in mind. It should include things like the right of substitution and clauses requiring you to repair bad work at your own expense. It should not contain things suggesting employment - holiday allowance, long notice periods or clauses that stop you working for other customers.

- Supply your own equipment, protective clothing and software

- Invest in your own training

- Invest in your own marketing and website

- Avoid being drawn into the customer's organisation in ways that make you appear to be an employee.

- Work from your own premises

- Make use of a substitute or helper

Nothing is clear cut however. There may good business reasons why, for example, you must use your customer's equipment or work in a certain way.

Since HMRC can assess working practices as well as the written contract, I normally ask my customer to sign a declaration at the end of a contract confirming the actual arrangements. This confirms equipment I have supplied, the task based nature of the work and whether the contract ceased early due to the task being completed.

Professional Opinion

It is your duty to take reasonable steps to decide if you are inside IR35. A number of companies offer to assess your assignment. I did this for one contract and paid £150 + VAT.

Not only does a professional opinion hopefully give you the correct answer, it shows you acted in good faith which should reduce penalties if an IR35 enquiry decides the professional opinion was wrong.

For the assessment I sent my contract and completed a detailed form about the actual working arrangements. This is important because HMRC can ignore the written contract and create their own version based on the actual arrangements if these are different.

IR35 insurance

The next step to reduce the risk from IR35 is to take out insurance. The most basic type covers the costs of being investigated, for example, lawyer and accountant's fees and time off work.

I joined a contractor's association which provided this insurance as a benefit of membership. It also covers time off work for jury duty and support during other tax or VAT investigations. My membership cost £248 and also provides online training resources and other membership benefits.

For the ultimate in IR35 protection some companies offer insurance that covers not only the investigation costs but also the extra tax you would pay back if you lost the case.

THE FUTURE

Recently introduced changes restrict travel expenses if caught by IR35.

The next step affects contractors working for public bodies. For these, the public body (rather than the contractor) will decide if the contract is within IR35. If inside, these businesses will not be allowed the normal 5% allowance to cover expenses.

The reason given is that they no-longer have the expense of deciding if IR35 applies. Other costs a small business might have do not seem to have been considered.

Other recent changes to discourage small limited companies are:

- The new 7.5% tax on dividends

- Withdrawal of the Employment Allowance if there is only one employee

- The "limited cost trader" rate for the VAT Flat Rate Scheme

Every time the Chancellor issues a budget or statement, watch out for a new anti-contractor rule.

9.   HOW TO INVOICE YOUR EXPENSES PROPERLY

If you have a contract to provide services, or even equipment, it may allow for the reimbursement of expenses at cost. This can be a minefield. Not only is it hard to understand the correct way to administer this, you then have the additional problem of convincing your customer to do things properly.

In an ideal world your contracts would be fixed price with a fat profit margin that covered your expenses. Unfortunately you are probably forced to take contracts which pay you for your time plus expenses at cost.

This chapter discusses the pitfalls, the dreadful lack of awareness you will encounter and finally how to charge expenses properly, without either wasting money or going to prison.

Being registered for VAT makes expenses particularly troublesome, especially if you are on the Flat Rate Scheme. It would be silly (and expensive) to change your business structure just to simplify your travel claims so let's learn how to do our expenses properly...

HOW NOT TO CHARGE EXPENSES

Suppose you are on a six month contract as an engineer to a large company. You understand IR35 (make sure you do) and are not caught. Your contract allows for expenses at cost and you have paid for some rail tickets, hotel bills and meals during a site visit.

Your customer (remember they are not your employer) may insist you fill in the same expenses form as their permanent employees. You supply receipts to go with the form and they pay that amount direct into your personal bank account. They may tell you that everyone does this, even the other twenty contractors they employ.

Just because everyone does something does not make it right. It is badly wrong in two ways.

Firstly, it clearly contradicts the premise that you are a business providing services outside of IR35. Businesses invoice customers for work done and products and services provided. Employees fill in expenses forms and get the money paid tax free into their bank account. If you are called to an IR35 enquiry which will you be?

Secondly it messes up your accounts. If you are not registered for VAT your company accounts will be missing transactions they should include but at least the tax you pay is probably right. If you are VAT registered you will actually be paying too little tax which will not go down well if Mr VAT man calls to see you.

SO HOW SHOULD IT WORK?

What you should do is invoice the customer for an amount which you agree is sufficient payment for the services you are providing. If you travel 200 miles on a train to do some fault finding at a remote substation then you are billing the customer for electrical work at a premium cost due to it being in an expensive place to get to. The customer's expectations may cause the amount billed to be exactly the same as the rail ticket price but that is just coincidence.

An example

Let's contrast life as an employee with that of a contractor in business for themselves.

An employee travels by rail and the ticket costs £100. They pay this with their own money and fill in an expenses form. Their employer gives them £100 tax free. The amount has to match. If they got £150 then not only would the employer be paying too much but the employee should be paying tax and National Insurance contributions on the extra £50 as wages.

The contractor is different. Suppose you travel to do some electrical work for a customer and buy a £100 rail ticket with your own money. The first step is that *your* company reimburses you. You receive exactly £100 tax free from your company and keep the receipt to prove to HMRC it was a genuine expenses claim.

You could create an expenses form for your own company. I find it easier instead to record such items as purchases by the company using the director's loan account. You could even buy direct from your company's current account and not involve your own money at all.

Your company now needs to charge the customer. This might be for the exact cost of the ticket but, provided the customer is happy to pay, could be for more or less. Since it is a bill for electrical work the amount is of no concern to HMRC. If your customer agrees to pay, there is no reason why you could not charge cost plus 10% for expenses or bill for the cost of rail travel but get a lift for free from a friend.

VAT

If you are not VAT registered then you give the customer an invoice for the agreed amount and everything is still quite simple.

If you are VAT registered things get tricky. Suppose you are registered on the Flat Rate Scheme paying 13.5% flat rate. Your company pays for a £100 rail ticket and a £100 hotel room. The travel is to a remote site to do some electrical work for the customer, a large, VAT registered business. Your contract gives a day rate for electrical work and stipulates expenses are paid at cost.

You invoice the electrical work at the agreed rate and add VAT at 20%. If that's not clear see the chapter on VAT. But what should you invoice for expenses? Here's how I do it.

Before we even consider how much "at cost" is we must understand what we are selling. Unless your business is a travel agent or a hotel you are not supplying your customer with rail tickets or hotel rooms.

In the above example you are supplying electrical engineering services. You should therefore charge VAT on your invoice at the rate for electrical engineering services which is 20%.

Now, how much is "at cost". Rail tickets are zero-rated for VAT so I would take a £100 rail ticket as costing £100. I would then invoice for this plus VAT at 20% which is £120.

Hotel room prices already include VAT so the £100 was actually £83.33 + £16.67 VAT. I would invoice for £83.33 and then add VAT which takes it back to £100.

MY CUSTOMER WON'T DO THAT

Hopefully everything makes sense so far. It is however, slightly counter-intuitive and raises a couple of strange problems.

The first is your customer. It took me a lot of work to understand how to invoice correctly. Your customer is not interested in getting your accounts right and just wants you to submit your expenses like their permanent employees and other contractors who don't know any better.

Even after you convince them that you need to submit an invoice because you are a contractor you may find them reluctant to pay 20% VAT on a rail ticket when rail travel is zero-rated. I found three things were useful to gain an acceptance of this by the customer:

- Remind them that they claim the VAT back anyway so it doesn't cost them any more

- Refer them to the excellent explanation on HMRC's website. Since the customer is not the one riding the train you are not selling a rail ticket. You are selling a day's electrical work and invoicing for the extra cost of providing that service at a remote site.

  (Search HMRC's website for "disbursements" and read the guidance notes: "VAT: costs or disbursements passed to customers". Disbursements are the rare situations where this principle does not apply)

- Get an email from your accountant confirming you are right. This will carry more weight with the customer's accounts people.

MAKING A LOSS?

Now you have invoiced correctly and got your customer to pay the invoices you may find the costs you pay and the money you receive do not match.

Take the above example and assume the value of the electrical work (labour only) was £1000.

On the Flat Rate Scheme you invoice this as £1200 (including VAT). When you do your VAT return you hand 13.5% of this to HMRC leaving you with £1038. A nice extra £38, courtesy of Mr VAT man in return for participating in his scheme.

With the £100 rail ticket the same thing happens. Your company invoices £120 and gets to keep £103.80. You invoiced at cost yet made £3.80 profit through Flat Rate Scheme magic!

Before you spend the £3.80 on a beer to toast your gift for accountancy you need to look at your hotel bill. This cost £100 but you only billed your client £100 (inc VAT). When you give 13.5% of this to the VAT man you are left with £86.50.

At first glance this seems wrong. It was bad enough telling your client they had to pay VAT on your zero-rated rail travel but now you are making random profits and losses.

The answer to most Flat Rate VAT puzzles is look at the overall purpose of the scheme. It is an approximate way of calculating VAT which small businesses may use to reduce administrative effort compared to the standard VAT scheme.

The reason you make £38 extra profit on your invoiced labour is to cover the VAT your business pays on accountancy fees, materials and just about everything else it buys. The two will not match exactly. If you make an extra profit you are small enough that the government doesn't mind. If you make a loss on your VAT then no one is forcing you to use the Flat Rate Scheme.

In this context the small gain on the rail ticket and the larger loss on the hotel are just part of the approximation. If you buy a lot of rail tickets you will gain. If you stay in a lot of hotels you will lose. Should the overall effect be negative then either get off the Flat Rate Scheme or insist your customer pays an additional admin charge above cost on expenses.

EXPENSES OUTSIDE OF THE FLAT RATE SCHEME

The above scenario is the most complex but is currently the most relevant for contractors. After 1st April 2017 many people may leave the Flat Rate Scheme due to the new 16.5% rate for limited cost traders.

On the standard VAT scheme expenses should be straightforward. The VAT collected is passed to HMRC, minus the VAT on any purchases. Invoicing for expenses would be as for the Flat Rate Scheme but all those approximations disappear, making your expenses exactly cover costs. Compared to the Flat Rate Scheme you might need to be more diligent in ensuring you receive proper VAT receipts on your purchases.

If you are not registered for VAT you can invoice for the full cost of expenses (£100 for the £83.33 + £16.67 VAT hotel room). Your customer will lose out however, since they will be unable to claim back the VAT you paid and you are passing this cost on to them.

10.   YEAR-END ACCOUNTING

Once you are comfortable with the routine operations of your business your final set of challenges come at the year-end. There are actually two years to consider, your company's financial year and the personal tax year.

As a company director you must:

- Register for personal self-assessment and submit a return

- Send an Annual Confirmation Statement to Companies House

- Prepare annual accounts for HMRC, Companies House and for certain stakeholders in your company

- Pay the taxes owed to HMRC

PERSONAL SELF-ASSESSMENT

The personal tax year is from the 6th April to the 5th April the following year. If you are a company director you must register for self-assessment, regardless of income level. You can only register after the end of the relevant financial year.

Register for self-assessment after the 5th April following becoming a director. You have until 31st January to submit your return and pay any extra tax owed.

Many accountants include director's self-assessment as a free extra service. You will need records of your income from the 6th April before your company started.

If you do not have an accountant you will need to register and complete your return via HMRC's website.

ANNUAL CONFIRMATION STATEMENT

Each year you must update Companies House with certain non-financial information, for example, the names of directors and the company's registered address. Unlike the financial accounts this must be sent within a few weeks of your year-end.

For company year-ends after 30th June 2016 you must submit a new document, the "Annual Confirmation Statement" which replaces the older "Annual Return".

This shows how quickly rules change. When I set up my business I learned about Annual Returns, only to find they had been replaced before the end of my first financial year.

When is the Annual Confirmation Statement due?

Companies House call the date one year from the incorporation of your company the "due date". Confusingly the "due date" is not the date that the return is due!

You must send your Annual Confirmation Statement within 14 days, starting from the due date. For my company, incorporated 12th November 2015, the due date was 12th

November 2016 and my confirmation statement was required by the 25th November 2016.

My Annual Confirmation Statement for the following year must to be submitted by the 25th November 2017.

How to complete the Annual Confirmation Statement

You may send your Annual Confirmation Statement electronically via the Companies House Website (**www.companieshouse.gov.uk**). This costs £13. If you insist on sending a paper copy it costs £40. Your accountant could also do it for a fee.

Before filing your statement you must register with the Companies House online filing system.

You must ensure that Companies House's records are already up to date for the following items:

- Company's officers

- Address of the company's registered office

- Address where the company's records are kept

If necessary update this information before producing your confirmation statement. The Annual Confirmation Statement only allows you to confirm these details are correct. It does not allow you to change them. You are supposed to have informed Companies House throughout the year as the changes happened.

Filing the Annual Confirmation Statement online is a simple affair as the Companies House website guides you through the process.

You will need to add details of Persons with Significant Control (PSC). Note that the date someone became a PSC cannot be earlier than 6th April 2016 when this new legislation took effect. Although I have been director and sole shareholder of my company since November 2015 I must say I became a Person with Significant Control on 6th April 2016.

You will also need to choose a Standard Industrial Categorisation (SIC) code to describe your business. The online form gives a link to the condensed list of codes which you must use. Despite codes for some very specialised activities (For example, space transportation and sweeping brush manufacture) the nearest fit I could find for the electrical design and commissioning I do was 71129 - Other Engineering Activities.

When you submit your statement, note the submission number. You will receive two emails, one to confirm your return has been received and a second to say it has been accepted (or rejected).

FINANCIAL END OF YEAR RETURN

At the end of the year you must produce Statutory Accounts.

These consist of:

- A balance sheet

- A profit and loss account

- Notes about the accounts

- A director's report

These must meet recognised accounting standards. For small companies and micro-entities they do not need to be checked by an external auditor.

These reports must be sent to:

- All share holders

- Anyone entitled to go to company general meetings

- HMRC

- Companies House

Accounting period and deadlines

HMRC require accounts every twelve months. If you start trading mid-month this means you must submit two sets of accounts after your first year. For example, I started my business on 12th November 2015. For my first year I submitted accounts for 12th November 2015 to 11th November 2016. I also submitted a second set of accounts to cover the two and a half weeks from 12th November 2016 to 30th November 2016.

In subsequent years I will only submit a single set, from 1st December to 30th November. You must pay Corporation Tax within 9 months and 1 day of the account period end. You have longer to produce the accounts but since you need the accounts to calculate the payment it is usual to submit the whole lot by this deadline. For your first year the small set of accounts covering less than a month are generally produced and submitted with the preceding year's.

Unlike HMRC, Companies House allow more than twelve months so do not need two separate sets for your first year.

You should file your first accounts within 21 months of your registration date and in subsequent years within nine months of your year-end. The exact rules are complex as there is scope to alter your year-end date. See the Companies House website in the unlikely event you want to do this.

Micro-entities

If your company meets any *two* of the following three conditions it is a "micro-entity".

- Turnover < £632 000

- Total of fixed and current assets < £316 000

- 10 employees or less

Micro-entities submit simpler accounts and do not need external auditors. The next step above a micro-entity is a "small company". Certain company structures and activities (for example insurance, banking and certain other financial services) are not allowed to be either small companies or micro-entities.

For micro-entities, Companies House allow the submission of abbreviated accounts. This avoids making your profit and loss account public. Full accounts still go to HMRC. Provided you do not need an auditor, it is possible to submit your full accounts to HMRC and abbreviated accounts to Companies House in one process.

End of year bookkeeping

There are a few bookkeeping items to consider as you reach the year end.

Watch out for expenses covering services outside of the period you are finalising. For example, my first set of accounts contained two annual insurance premiums, one of which was a payment in advance the following year. You may also have expense items which HMRC does not allow for the calculation of Corporation Tax. You need to flag up these things to your accountant or make the appropriate bookkeeping corrections yourself.

HMRC give a small allowance for the use of your home as an office which can be claimed without actual proof of bills. Currently this is £208 per year and my accountant included it before preparing my accounts.

When your accounts for the year are complete it is necessary to finalise the year in QuickFile. This creates journal entries to record your retained earnings. These are profits not yet distributed as dividends and form part of your dividend calculations in subsequent years. My accountant finalised my accounts but there are instructions in the QuickFile documentation to do it yourself.

Producing the accounts

Actually producing the accounts themselves is beyond the scope of this book. The budget accountancy package I use includes production and submission of my annual accounts.

A cheaper alternative is a "check and file" service in which you produce your own accounts but an accountant checks and submits them.

Should you wish to file your own accounts without using an accountant, HMRC's website includes an online tool to allow you to enter them.

Paying up

You can pay your Corporation Tax via bank transfer from your company's account using the information on the payment slips that HMRC will post to you. For your first year there will be two payments (with different payment references) corresponding to the two accounting periods. By adding Corporation Tax to your HMRC online services account you can check how much you owe. HMRC's site also describes other methods of payment.

You can pay your personal self-assessment bill via HMRC's website using a debit card without logging in to online services. Remember that you pay this bill, not your company.

11.   SETTING UP A WEBSITE

While this book covers your company accounts you probably also need a website. Like accountancy I had to learn this from scratch so I think it is worthwhile sharing how to do it.

I wanted to pay the minimum but have something more professional than a free site. To see the end result visit **www.JERelectrical.com**.

REQUIREMENTS

I only needed a very simple site. It would provide brief information about my company, allow me to operate a professional email address and provide a website to put on my business cards. Rather than just a few static pages I also wanted the ability to add blog pages. These would make my site more interesting to visitors, showcase my talents and potentially create extra revenue opportunities.

My specification:

- I needed something that looked professional.

- I wanted my own domain name.

- I wanted some static pages (the ones telling you about my company).

- I also wanted blog pages (the articles).

- I didn't want adverts (unless the advertisers were paying me).

- I'm no expert in web design so I wanted something quick and simple.

- I needed an email account with my own domain address (**sales@JERelectrical.com**).

- I wanted to keep costs low.

To achieve this you will need to do the following:

- Register a domain name (You hire an address like **www.JERelectrical.com** by the year)

- Pay for web hosting (Space on a computer somewhere where all your pages live)

- Obtain software to create and operate the site. When a visitor views pages they are interacting with a program running on the hosting company's computer.

- (optional) Pay to keep your personal details private when you register

- (optional - depending on your web host) Hire space on a server for your email account

It is advisable to register the domain name (the address) and the hosting (the place where your website files are stored) separately. That way if you fall out with your webhost it is easy to hire another. You reconfigure your domain name to point at the new host and there is nothing the old host can do about it.

Things I rejected

Some deals offer combined registration and hosting with your first year free. The catch is that, after the first year, it gets a lot more expensive. Since your domain name is registered by them they can charge you an exit fee if you wish to change provider but keep your domain name.

Even where you are not trapped in this way, many providers offer an artificially low cost at first with the long term price hidden in small print. This makes it very time consuming to compare prices.

Another option is to use free hosting. If you want to play with websites for fun this is fine but I wanted something more polished. The catch with free hosting:

- Your domain name includes the supplier, for example **www.jerelectrical.wordpress.com**.

- You get adverts.

- There are restrictions on the features you can use within the website.

- There are commercial restrictions. For example, you might not be permitted to display your own paid adverts.

So what did I choose?

I registered my domain name with **www.123-reg.co.uk** on recommendation. It cost me £10/year.

I also paid £5/year for the privacy option. For names ending .uk or .co.uk EU law makes this free to individuals but not companies.

For web hosting I compared many providers. In the end I went with **www.tsohost.com**. There was nothing as cheap for a really small site. The package I chose cost me £15/year for the following:

- 500 MB storage (the amount of pages and photos you have)

- 5 GB bandwidth (the data your visitors download each month as they look at the pages)

- The ability to host your email for free (this uses up some of the 500MB)

This is a very cheap package and only suits a small site. You can pay them more for extra bandwidth and storage if your site takes off.

For software I choose WordPress. It's free. It's incredibly widely used and it supports both blog posts and static pages. You could instead obtain different software or use something provided by your webhosting company.

SETTING UP THE WEBSITE

Having made the above choices, this is how to set everything up. I'll base the explanation on 123 Reg and Tsohost but other providers will be similar.

Pay for your name and hosting

First go to **www.123-reg.co.uk** and enter domain names for your site until you find one which is available and suits your budget. Select the privacy option if you want. Pay for this domain name.

Next go to **www.tsohost.com** and pay for a hosting package. It is worth checking my website (**www.JERelectrical.com**) as I have a link and code which will give you a discount.

Set up your website

When you pay for the above items you will receive emails from each company with login information to their respective control panels.

Log into the control panel for 123 Reg and enter the server details which tsohost.com have sent you. This will point the address registered at 123 Reg to the server (at Tsohost). The screen shot below shows the three lines you must type to tell 123 Reg who your hosting is with.

Figure 4.   Setting up DNS addresses on 123 Reg control panel

Nameserver 1	ns1.tsohost.co.uk	Required
Nameserver 2	ns3.tsohost.co.uk	Required
Nameserver 3	ns2.tsohost.co.uk	
Nameserver 4		

Now you can close the 123 Reg control panel and use the link on the Tsohost email to log into the Tsohost control panel.

Tsohost will email you simple instructions on creating your website. You go into their control panel and click "Add website". Type in your registered web address (for example **jerelectrical.com**).

For operating system select Linux unless you have a good reason to do otherwise. Don't worry if you've never run Linux and have only used Windows. Linux runs in the background and you will still be able to develop your website with no Linux knowledge.

Once you have created your website enter "Manage Website" and you will see many options as shown in figure 5.

Figure 5. The Tsohost "Manage Website" control panel

Set up your email

Tsohost let you use your web hosting as an email server. Select "Email Accounts" and create an email address containing your new domain name, for example sales@jerelectrical.com. You can also add an alias (a different email address that goes to the same place). You can check your emails online using a website called Gridhost. Tsohost's emails include links and instructions for this. Alternatively you could set up Microsoft Outlook on your PC to log into your emails.

Now your email is done let's get back to the website. In the "Manage Website" section go to "Application Options" at the bottom and select "Install Applications". Find WordPress and click the button for one click install.

A summary of the set up so far

So far you have registered a web address via a domain registrar. You have also rented space at a web hosting company and pointed your web address to it. You have set up an email server using a bit of the web hosting space and you have installed the WordPress software on it to handle your website. When you install WordPress you will get login details for WordPress administrator access to your site. Be sure to note all the passwords and usernames. Here is the list of things you can now log into:

Account	Purpose
Control panel with your domain name company	Paying for / administering your web address Pointing your domain name to the location of your site on the web host computer
Control panel with your web hosting company	Paying for / administering you web hosting package Creating your initial website shell and installing WordPress to run it Possibly setting up email Looking at statistics for visitors to your site
Email hosting (if separate from your web hosting supplier)	Paying for / administering your email hosting package

Account	Purpose
Your company email account	Sending and receiving emails (I access this via the Gridhost website)
Your website as WordPress administrator	Alter the structure of your site, add content, change settings and themes and approve comments on blog posts Access this by adding "/wp-admin" to the end of your web address in your browser, for example: **www.JERelectrical.com/wp-admin**

WHAT NOW?

You are now the owner of a website. It shows a few test blog posts from WordPress and runs their standard WordPress theme. You can even add a few posts and comments and type your newly rented domain name into a web browser to admire them.

At this stage I became somewhat dispirited. Setting up the website was easy but at first I could not see how to change this demo website into something useful with pages looking the way I wanted.

The breakthrough for me was adding a new theme. A theme is not just a cosmetic way to change the fonts and colours. Adding a theme allowed me to transform my site into something with a proper structure. The small selection of pre-installed themes did not suit my tastes so I downloaded an alternative one.

To change theme log into your website as administrator (wp-admin) and select:

Appearance --> Themes --> Add new

You can pick from hundreds of free themes. After trying a few and reading reviews I went for Parabola. It is free, very flexible and if you don't mind your site looking a bit like mine I can recommend it. You can always change it later.

WordPress is based on two types of document - pages (the fixed pages accessed via menus) and blogs (my articles). The settings within the theme allow you to alter the appearance of the site and Parabola has extra settings that give you more freedom than WordPress normally allows.

There are also things called widgets which you can drag to parts of your page. These are useful tools to create a functioning website without any programming. For example, my site displays a list of my latest articles using a widget.

I cannot describe everything here but the above paragraphs cover the main points to get you started.

EXTRA TIPS

When you are editing a page or post you can switch between "visual" or "text" using the tab at the top right. Visual shows what you actually see on the website. Text shows the code that creates the correct formatting. I suggest you use visual most of the time. It lets you add things like photographs, bold text or headings without understanding how it is done.

If you switch to text you can see the code behind the document you have typed. You can then edit it directly. Search the web for "html" to learn more about these codes.

As an example paste the following code in the text view to get a table.

```
<table border="1">
<tbody>
<tr>
<th>Animal</th>
<th>Colour</th>
</tr>
<tr>
<td>Mouse</td>
<td>Grey</td>
</tr>
<tr>
<td>Sheep</td>
<td>White</td>
</tr>
<tr>
<td>Horse</td>
<td>Brown</td>
</tr>
</tbody>
</table>
```

Click the "Visual" tab and you should see the following:

Animal	Colour
Mouse	Grey
Sheep	White
Horse	Brown

Look at the code and you'll soon see how to alter it to get any table you want.

Have fun with your new website. Although I've based the examples on Tsohost, most hosts will allow you to install WordPress although the install may involve an extra step if the host does not provide one click install.

12.   FINAL THOUGHTS

I hope you have found this book useful. Virtually everything covered was something I learned in the first year of running my business. My aim was to provide this information in adequate detail to run your company accounts, yet without the distracting side issues of a more comprehensive accountancy book.

During my first year I have discovered a few other things which I'd like to share.

The first is just how much effort is needed to run a business. Initially I spent a huge amount of time researching how to do things. Now that I understand most of the tasks, I still need a few hours each week to issue invoices, record expenses and do my payroll and VAT returns.

The second is just how complex the rules for businesses are. Accountancy is as much about knowing the regulations as handling the figures.

The third is how messy the whole system is. I assumed things would be black and white but so many decisions involve making a judgement and hoping you can later show it was reasonable. I suspect there are thousands of people whose accounts are full of errors and are unaware.

The final surprise for me was how quickly rules change. Of the things I learned in my first months, many are outdated just one year later.

Accountancy for UK Contractors

In a year I have seen:

- The abolition of the 10% dividend tax credit and its replacement with a new 7.5% dividend tax

- The abolition of the Employment Allowance for single person companies

- Additional restrictions on travel expenses for those within IR35

- The replacement of the Annual Return with the new Annual Confirmation Statement

- The planned changes to VAT for limited cost traders on the Flat Rate Scheme

- A plan to make public bodies responsible for deciding if their contractors are inside IR35

- A plan to remove the 5% expenses allowance for IR35 contractors to public bodies

Good luck with your business and be sure to keep up to date.

If you have enjoyed this book, it would be most appreciated if you could go online and leave a short review.

APPENDIX A.   USEFUL CONTACTS

My Company Website

James E Richardson (Electrical) Limited	Be sure to visit my website which includes:
www.JERelectrical.com	<ul><li>Information related to this book</li><li>Short articles on business, engineering, practical hobbies and other interesting topics</li><li>Details of my electrical engineering business</li><li>My business contact details</li></ul> If you are making a website, it also shows what can be done with minimal effort using the tips in Chapter 11.

Businesses I Have Used

The following are businesses I have used myself and can recommend. While you may find others, I hope these provide a useful starting point and will save you some time.

IR35 assessment and insurance

Abbey Tax www.abbeytax.co.uk	I used Abbey Tax to check the IR35 status of a contract. They also offer various forms of IR35 insurance.
IPSE The Association of Independent Professionals and the Self-Employed www.ipse.co.uk	IPSE is a contractor association which offers tax investigation insurance as a member benefit. They also provide training materials, advice and events.

Limited company registration

Rapid Formations www.rapidformations .co.uk	These are the agents I used to register my company.

Low cost accountancy

Cheap Accounting www.cheapaccounting .co.uk	This is the low cost accountancy service I chose when I started my business.

Insurance

Kingsbridge www.kingsbridge .co.uk	This company provided me with a contractor's insurance package covering professional indemnity and public liability.

Cloud Based Accounting Software

QuickFile www.quickfile.co.uk	This is the cloud based accountancy software I use. It is free for very small businesses with up to 1000 transactions a year. I have about 800 so do not pay.

Website

123 Reg www.123-reg.co.uk	This company registered my domain name.
Tsohost www.tsohost.com	I used Tsohost as my web host. They were the cheapest I could find for a very small site and had straightforward pricing. See my website for a discount code.

Government Organisations

The only reason you are reading this book is the government's need to ensure you pay the correct taxes. Otherwise you could forget about accountancy and not keep any records at all.

You will deal with many government agencies. Some are excellent with helpful staff and efficient computer systems that save you time. Others are rather frustrating.

Government Gateway

www.gov.uk/log-in-register-hmrc-online-services	Often referred to as government "online services" you can set up two Government Gateway accounts.
	Set up one "business account" and use it for your VAT returns, payroll and Corporation Tax. Then set up a second as an "individual" and use it to view your self-assessment.
	The Government Gateway accounts are characterised by the 12 digit username you are given, along with warnings that you must write it down as it will not be shown again.
	Initially I only used Government Gateway for my VAT since my accountant dealt with other matters using an "agent" account. It is possible to set up your own account to see what your agent has been up to. There is no issue with viewing your data yourself, even if you have an agent doing the work

HMRC

https://www.gov.uk /government/organisations /hm-revenue-customs	HMRC (Her Majesty's Revenue and Customs) collect taxes. Their website is a valuable source of information. Be warned that the information (and the law) change frequently. I spent my first few months studying the rules only to find the website had been updated and many things had changed. HMRC collect VAT, Income Tax, National Insurance and Corporation Tax. To help them check you are paying enough, you must send them payroll information, VAT returns, annual accounts and personal self-assessments.

Government Verify

It is not possible to go directly to Government Verify from an external site but you can reach it by choosing "sign in with UK.GOV Verify" on this page: https://www.gov.uk/personal -tax-account	This new system lets you look at things like your personal National Insurance history and Income Tax code. The overlap in purpose between this and the individual Government Gateway account can be confusing.

Companies House

www.gov.uk/government /organisations/companies-house	Companies House register companies and ensure they follow the rules. They do not collect taxes but do charge small fees when you interact with them. At the end of each year you must send them an Annual Confirmation Statement and accounts.

The Pensions Regulator

www.thepensionsregulator.gov.uk and www.tpr.gov.uk/confirm-duty	If you register for PAYE, The Pensions Regulator will write to you about providing an employee pension scheme. If you are a director and the only employee you can opt out of the requirement to provide a workplace pension.

APPENDIX B.   COMPANY DETAILS

You will find it useful to record the following items in one place but please keep this list safe as it contains sensitive information. You should not write down your passwords but even a tiny hint will help you remember them.

See my website **www.JERelectrical.com** to download an electronic copy.

<u>About Your Company</u>

Company name:	
Company registration date:	
Company registration number:	
Registered office address:	
Names and addresses of directors:	
SIC code / description (from condensed list):	
Company UTR number (for Corporation Tax):	

HMRC gateway details (Company)

Username (12 digit Number):	
Password hint:	

VAT registration

VAT number:	
VAT registration date:	

Are you on the Flat Rate Scheme?	
Cash or accrual accounting for VAT?	

Flat rate sector description:	
Flat rate for this sector:	
Your flat rate: (including 1% first year reduction if applicable)	

VAT period end dates: (Choose one line)	End Jan, Apr, Jul, Oct End Feb, May, Aug, Nov End Mar, Jun, Sep, Dec
Direct debit set up for VAT payment to HMRC?	Reference:

Companies House Account

Email used for registration:	
Authorisation code:	
Password hint:	

PAYE registration

PAYE registration number:	
Are you registered as a director for PAYE (NI paid at end of year)?	
Have you registered as exempt from providing a workplace pension?	

Accounting/Bookkeeping software

Software name / website:	
Account number/Username:	
Password hint:	

Annual returns and accounts

Date Annual Confirmation Statement is next due:	
Date accounts and payment of Corporation Tax are due:	

Company bank account

Account name:	
Bank name:	
Bank address:	
Account number:	
Sort code:	
Internet banking web address:	
Username: (if applicable)	
Password hint:	

Company Insurance

Policy number:	
Type: (delete as required)	Professional indemnity Public liability Employer's liability
Insurer:	
Username: (if applicable)	
Password hint:	

Your company website and email

Domain Name

Domain name:	
Domain registrar:	
Domain registrar web address / contact details:	
Your email address used when setting up domain name: (used for password reset, payment reminders, etc.)	
Domain registrar username (if applicable):	
Domain registrar password hint:	

Web hosting

Web hosting provider:	
Web hosting web address / contact details:	
Your email address used when setting up web hosting: (used for password reset, payment reminders, etc)	
Web hosting username (if applicable):	
Password hint:	

Company email (set up)

Company email address(es):	
Email hosting provider (if different to web host):	
Your email address used when setting up email hosting: (used for password reset, payment reminders, etc.)	
Password hint:	

Company email (reading / sending)

Website address for reading / sending email:	
Password hint:	

Website / WordPress administration

Company website administrator username: Access admin page by adding **/wp_admin** to your website address	
Password hint:	

Other online accounts

Description / Web address:	Username: / Email used to register:	Password hint:

Description / Web address:	Username / Email used to register:	Password hint:

About You

National Insurance Number:	
Your personal UTR Number: (as a person for self-assessment)	

HMRC gateway (Personal, non-business account)

Username (12 digit Number):	
Password hint:	

Government Verify

Email used to register:	
Registration company:	
Password hint:	

Contact phone numbers:

Insurer:	
Accountant:	
Bank:	
Formation company:	

ABOUT THE AUTHOR

James Richardson studied electronics at the University of York. He then spent ten years in the steel industry, working on installation and maintenance of heavy electrical equipment.

He qualified as a Chartered Electrical Engineer and later moved to Scotland to work on the Pelamis wave energy device.

In 2015 he set up James E Richardson (Electrical) Limited, an electrical engineering business, based in Edinburgh.

Notes

Printed in Great Britain
by Amazon